WHO TELLS THE TRUTH?

logical puzzles to make you think

Adam Case

D0784481

tarquin publications

CE

Published by tarquin publications
> 99 Hatfield Road
> St Albans
> England
> AL1 4JL
> www.tarquinbooks.com

Copyright © Adam Case, 2006

ISBN: 978-0-906212-77-6

Design: Jane Adams
Drawings: Annabelle Curtis
Production: HadleyMarketing

Printing: Ashford Colour Press, UK

Contents

The Two Families

The first set of logical puzzles introduces the members of both the Troo family and the Fals family, who have very different standards of behaviour. Members of the Troo family always tell the truth in every statement that they make and members of the Fals family always lie.

By looking at any person, you cannot tell which family he or she belongs to. The puzzle is to think about the statements that are made and then decide who is telling the truth and who is lying. From that you will be able to answer the question.

TROOS ALWAYS TELL THE TRUTH
FALS ALWAYS LIE

1   The first people you meet are Alan and Bert. Alan makes the
    following statement:
        Alan: Both of us are from the Fals family.
    Which family does Alan belong to? What about Bert?

2   Next you meet Christine and Daphne. From Christine's statement,
    work out which family Daphne comes from.
        Christine: Exactly one of us is from the Fals family.

3   The next two people you meet are Ernie and Fred. From what Ernie
    says, work out Fred's family.
        Ernie: We are both from the same family.

4 Next you come across Gertrude and Hilda. Work out Hilda's family from Gertrude's statement.

   Gertrude: Exactly one of us is from the Troo family.

   Is it possible to say which family Gertrude belongs to?

5 Now you find Ian and John. Ian makes the following statement:

   Ian: At least one of us is from the Troo family.

   What can you say about Ian and John?

6 Karen and Laura are next. From Karen's statement can you say anything about the families they are from?

   Karen: I am from the Fals family and Laura is from the Troo family.

7 Mark and Neil are the last people you meet. Mark makes the following statement:

> *Mark:* It is not the case that Neil and I are both from the Troo family.

Which families do Mark and Neil come from?

The solutions to THE TWO FAMILIES puzzles are on page 64.

More about the Families

In each of the first group of puzzles, only one person made a statement. In this second group, statements are made by two people and sometimes by as many as three. Since each person is a member of either the Troo family or the Fals family, each statement can be true or false. In each puzzle all the people may belong to the same or different families.

Since the names are not important, it seems simpler to refer to the people simply by capital letters, working consecutively through the alphabet.

 TROOS ALWAYS TELL THE TRUTH
FALS ALWAYS LIE

1   You come across A and B. They make the following statements:
      A: I belong to the Troo family.
      B: We are both from the same family.
    Which family do A and B belong to?

2   You next see C and D. Work out as much as you can about their
    families from the following statements:
      C: We are from different families.
      D: C is from the Fals family.

3   What can you say about the families of E and F from the
    following statements?
      E: We are both from the Troo family.
      F: E is not from the Fals family.

4　Next you see G and H who make the following statements:

     G:　I am from the Troo family.

     H:　G is from the Fals family.

What can you work out about these two?

5　The following two people you meet are I and J.
They make the following statements:

     I:　We are from different families.

     J:　We are from the same family and I is lying.

Which families do I and J belong to?

6　Let us suppose that, when you met I and J in the previous puzzle,
they made statements as follows:

     I:　We are from different families.

     J:　We are from the same family and I am lying.

Which families do I and J belong to this time? This puzzle may
seem to be a repeat of the previous one, but look carefully at the
changed wording.

7   K and L make the following statements:

    K: It is not the case that I am from the Troo family and L is also from the Troo family.

    L: K is from the Fals family.

What can you say about the families of these two?

8   Not surprisingly, the next two people you meet are called M and N. They say the following:

    M: If I am from the Troo family than N is also from the Troo family.

    N: We are both from the same family.

Which family does M belong to? What about N? Is N's statement necessary in solving the puzzle?

9   You next see O and P. They make the following statements:

    O: Exactly one of these two statements is true.

    P: Exactly one of these two statements is false.

Is it true that both O and P must come from the same family?

10 In the next four puzzles three people instead of just two are talking.
    Q, R and S say the following:

    Q: R is from the Fals family.
    R: S is from the Troo family.
    S: Either I am from the Fals family or I am from the Troo family.
    Which families are the three from?

11 T, U and V are next. From their statements, can you work out the
    families that they are from?

    T: U is a different family from V.
    U: V is from the Fals family.
    V: At least one of us is from the Fals family.

12 You see W, X and Y. They say the following:

    W: X is from the Fals family.
    X: We are all from the same family.
    Y: At least one of us is from the Fals family.
    Which one comes from which family?

12

13 ZA and ZB have double initials, but they are still from the same families as Z and the others. They make these statements:

Z: At least one of us is from the Troo family.

ZA: That's a lie!

ZB: If ZA said "That is true" then you couldn't work out which family he belonged to.

When solving this puzzle you must assume that ZA was referring to Z's statement when he said "That's a lie!" This puzzle is quite difficult to solve.

14 This is another quite difficult puzzle. From these statements made by ZC, ZD and ZE, can you work out which families that they came from (if it is possible)?

>ZC: ZD and ZE belong to the same family.
>
>ZD: ZC and ZE belong to the same family.
>
>ZE: I do not belong to the same family as ZD.

The remaining four puzzles in this chapter are also about 3 members of the two families but only the first two will make statements. You have to work out the families that the silent third person comes from using the statements of the other two people.

15 ZF and ZG make the following statements about themselves and ZH:

>ZF: Exactly one of the three of us is from the Fals family.
>
>ZG: ZI and ZK are from different families.

Which family is ZH from?

16 From the two statements made by ZI and ZJ, can you work out
which family that ZK is from?

    ZI: ZJ is from the Troo family.

    ZJ: ZI and ZK are from different families.

17 ZL, ZM and ZN are next. ZL and ZM say the following:

    ZL: ZM is from the Fals family.

    ZM: ZL and ZN are from the same family.

Again, this puzzle is similar to the previous one. I have changed
the word "Troo" to "Fals" in ZL's statement and "different" to "the
same" in ZM's statement. Which family is ZN from?

18 ZO and ZP say the following about themselves and ZQ:

    ZO: All three of us are from the Troo family.

    ZP: All three of us are from the Fals family.

Which family is ZQ from? With so little information, can you also
say which families ZO and ZP are from?

The solutions to MORE ABOUT THE FAMILIES start on page 64.

16

18

Classes 1, 2 and 3

The puzzles in this group all concern the members of three classes in a certain school. Members of class 1 always tell the truth, so every statement they make is true. Members of class 2 always lie, so every statement is false. Members of class 3 can tell the truth or lie as they prefer at the time.

For each puzzle one person from each class is present. Everyone in the school knows who belongs to each class, but other people cannot tell them apart except by thinking about what thcy say. To solve the puzzle you have first to decide who is telling the truth and who is lying. Hopefully it is then just a short step to answering the question.

CLASS 1 TELLS THE TRUTH
CLASS 2 TELLS LIES
CLASS 3 LIES OR TELLS THE TRUTH

1 You meet A, B and C. They say the following:
   A: Of these three statements, exactly two are true.
   B: If I am from class 2 then A is from class 3.
   C: I am not from class 1.
   Which classes are A, B and C from?

2 D, E and F are next. From their statements, work out which classes
   they are from:
   D: E is from class 3.
   E: D is from class 1.
   F: I am from class 3.

3 G, H and I make the following statements
   G: I am from class 2.
   H: I am from class 3.
   I: G is from class 3.
   Which classes are they from?

4   J, K and L are next. They say the following:

    J: I am not from class 3.

    K: J is not from class 3.

    L: J's statement has the same truth value as K's statement.

Which classes are the three from? You must know that, when L said "has the same truth value as" he meant that J's statement and K's statement are both false or both true.

5   The next three people to make statements are M, N and O. Which classes are they from?

    M: Of myself and N, just one of us is from class 2.

    N: O is from class 1.

    O: M is from class 2.

6   P, Q and R are next. They make the following statements:

    P: Q is from class 3 and I am from class 2.

    Q: P is from class 1 and R is from class 3.

    R: I am from class 1.

I do not ask you to find out which class each person is from because this puzzle would not be possible. However, you can find out which class R is from and whether Q's statement is true or false.

7   S, T and U say the following:
>   *S:* T is from class 3.
>   *T:* I am from class 3.
>   *U:* I am from class 3.

Who is a member of which class?

8   Suppose S, T and U had said the following:
>   *S:* T is from class 3.
>   *T:* I am from class 3.
>   *U:* I am not from class 3.

This puzzle is very similar to the previous one. The only difference is in U's statement but that is sufficient to change the answer completely.

9   V, W and X are the last three. They each make statements
    as follows:
        V: I am from class 1.
        W: I am from class 2.
        X: I am from class 3.
    This puzzle is quite easy but it often catches people out. What class
    is each person from?

The solutions to the CLASSES 1, 2 AND 3 puzzles are on page 66.

Whose Room is it?

In this group of puzzles the Troo and Fals families all went to a holiday village on a small island. Each adult had his or her room, which was numbered, but because the two families were friends, they spent a lot of time visiting each other.

I went on holiday to the same village and thought it would be interesting to find out the room number of everyone. The Troos always tell the truth, but the members of the Fals family still always lie. All of them know which family everyone comes from, but I could not tell them apart except by thinking about what they said.

Two or three people were present in each room that I visited, always including the owner. The puzzle is to find out from their statements who is telling the truth and who is lying. Once that is established, it should be a simple matter to determine which room it was and which family he or she belonged to.

There is also an interesting puzzle about their room numbers.

TROOS ALWAYS TELL THE TRUTH
FALS ALWAYS LIE

1   The first room I went to was number 2. A and B were there. They
    said the following:
    A: Both of us are from the Fals family.
    B: I occupy this room.
    Whose room is it? Is it the occupier of the Troos or the Fals family?

2   C and D are in the second room. They made the following
    statements:
    C: Exactly one of us is from the Troo family.
    D: C is staying in this room.
    Whose room number is it and is she telling the truth? This time the
    room number was number 16.

3 I went next to number 29. E and F were there and said the following:

> *E:* At least one of us is from the Troo family and this is my room.
>
> *F:* Both of us are from the Fals family and it is my room.

Whose room is it? Can you work out which family the owner is from?

4 The next room was number 4. The two people in there, G and H, said the following:

> *G:* At least one of us from the Fals family and H is staying in this room.
>
> *H:* G is from the Troo family.

Whose room is it and which family is the occupant from?

5 The next room I visited was room number 17. I and J were there and made the following statements:

> *I:* We are either both from the Fals family or both from the Troo family.
>
> *J:* This room is mine.

Is it really J's room? Is he telling the truth?

6   K, L and M were in the next room which was number 7. They said the following:

 K: This is my room.

 L: This is my room.

 M: I am from the same family as L.

K and L cannot be telling the truth! Whose room is number 7 and which family is the occupant from?

7   The final room that I visited was number 15. N, O and P were there. They each made a statement:

 N: This room belongs to P.

 O: I am from the same family as P.

 P: The room belongs to N.

Whose room is it and which family is he or she from?

Is it possible that I and P are brother and sister?

8   I was about to visit room 11 when I realised that there was a
     pattern to the answers so far. Simply by looking at the room number
     I was able to tell whether the occupant was a Troo or a Fals.
     What was the rule and what family did the occupant of room 11
     belong to?

         There were 30 rooms in the holiday village, numbered from 1 to
         30. I was staying in room 1 and the other 29 rooms were all
         occupied by the Troo or Fals families. How many of each were
         there?

The solutions to the WHOSE ROOM IS IT? puzzles are on page 67.

Who does it Belong to?

This group of puzzles brings us back to the pupils of classes 1, 2 and 3 who are now arguing over various objects which have been found in the school. The pupils of class 1 still always tell the truth as before. The pupils of class 2 always lie and the pupils of class 3 sometimes lie and sometimes tell the truth. One person from each class is present in each discussion.

The additional piece of information is that the owner of the object always lies. However, in spite of this extra difficulty it is still possible to find out who does own it. That is the puzzle.

CLASS 1 TELLS THE TRUTH
CLASS 2 TELLS LIES
CLASS 3 LIES OR TELLS THE TRUTH
THE OWNER ALWAYS LIES

1   A, B and C are talking about a ruler. They say the following:
    A: This ruler belongs to me.
    B: A is lying.
    C: Of these three statements,
        exactly two are true.
    Who owns the ruler?

2   D, E and F make the following the statements:
    D: The football belongs to me.
    E: D is from class 1.
    F: The football belongs to E.
    Who owns the football?

3   G, H and I are talking about a pencil. Who owns it?
    G: I own the pencil.
    H: Exactly one of these three statements is false.
    I: H is from class 2.

4   J, K and L are talking about an apple. From their statements, can
    you work out who owns it?
        J: The apple belongs to L.
        K: J is from class 1.
        L: J's statement is false.

5   M, N and O say the following:
        M: The book belongs to O.
        N: The book belongs to O.
        O: The book is not mine.
    Who owns the book? You are not able to solve this puzzle with
    that information only so I will tell you that more people are telling
    the truth than are lying. Now it is really easy.

6   P, Q and R are talking about a lunch box. Whose it is?
        P: At least one of these three statements is false.
        Q: The lunch box belongs to P.
        R: The lunch box does not belong to P.

The solutions to the WHO DOES IT BELONG TO? puzzles are on page 68.

34

The Tals and the Froos

The well-known families of the Troos and the Fals began to intermarry and to have children. These children shared the characteristics of their parents as other children do. It was found that when a Troo man married a Fals woman, their sons always told the truth and their daughters always lied. When a Fals man married a Troo woman it was the daughters who told the truth and the sons who lied.

Usually a family takes its surname from the father, but that would cause problems in these families. Females from a family with a Troo father would carry the name Troo until they married but would tell lies. Likewise boys with the surname Fals would tell the truth. This would be most confusing. The answer was to use the surname TALS for the children with a Troo father and FROO for children with a Fals father. Hence Tals males and Froo females always tell the truth and Tals females and Froo males always lie.

Now for the puzzles!

TALS MALES TELL THE TRUTH
TALS FEMALES LIE
FROO MALES LIE
FROO FEMALES TELL THE TRUTH

1 The first speaker, A, says the following:

   A: I am a Froo male.

   Is A male or female and which family does he or she come from?

2 B, the second person, says the following:

   B: I am a Tals female.

   What can you say about B?

3 C is third. C makes the following statement:

   C: I am not a Tals male.

   Which family does C come from? Is C male or female.

4   From the simple statement below, work out as much about D as you can.

    D: I am from the Tals family.

5   E says the following:

    E: I am female.

What can you say about E?

6   F makes the following statement:

    F: I am from the Froo family.

What can you say about F?

7   G is next and says the following:

    G: I am male.

Do you really need to work this out? What can you say about G?

The last three puzzles of this group are about two people making statements instead of just one. Work out the sex and the family of each.

8   H and I are speaking next. You know that one of them is female and one is male. They say the following:

      H: I am from the Tals family.

      I: H is not from the Tals family.

What can you say about H and I?

9   From the following statements made by J and K, what can you say about them? You know that they are both male.

      J: I am female.

      K: J is from the Tals family.

10 L and M are next. You know that one of them is male and one is female. What can you say about them from their statements?

      L: M is from the Tals family.

      M: We are both from the Tals family.

The solutions to THE TALS AND THE FROOS puzzles are on page 68.

John and his Twins

This group of puzzles is all about asking the right question. There are only two people present, John and his identical twin. It is difficult for anyone to tell them apart and they like to play a rather mischievous game. Each morning when they wake up they decide who is to tell the truth for that day and who is to lie. They keep their decision secret from everyone else. Actually, even if you knew that John was lying, you still wouldn't be able to see at a glance which one was John.

IF JOHN LIES HIS TWIN TELLS THE TRUTH
IF JOHN TELLS THE TRUTH HIS TWIN LIES

1   You meet the two brothers together and you wish to find out which of them is John. You may only ask one question of one of them, which has to be answered by either. "Yes" or "No". What is the simplest question that you can ask?

2   On another occasion you meet both the brothers together and this time you wish to find out if John is telling the truth that day. Again you may only ask one of the brothers one question that has to be answered by either "Yes" or "No". What is the simplest question that you can ask this time?

3   For once you know for certain which twin is John. You ask him a single question in order to find out if his brother's name is Mark or Marcus. He answers with the word "No" and you are then certain that his brother's name is Mark. What is the question?

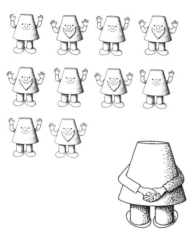

A barber who lives in a small town shaves all the inhabitants who do not shave themselves and he never shaves any inhabitants who do shave themselves. He is the only barber in town and does not grow a beard.
Does the barber shave himself or not?

4   John and Mark have relatives who each fall into one of three different categories. They either tell the truth all the time, always lie or answer consecutive questions alternatively with the truth or a lie. Their mother falls into one of these categories. What two questions could you ask her to find out which category she belongs to. She can only answer "Yes" or "No".

Having discovered that, can you always find out which twin is John by asking a third question? She of course can distinguish between her sons.

The solutions to the JOHN AND HIS TWINS puzzles are on page 69.

Talking to the Tals and Froos

On page 4 you were introduced to the Tals and the Froos and all those puzzles were in the usual form of a question or problem to which you had to find the answer. This group of puzzles in the other way round.

You need some information, but you do not know whether the person you are talking to is lying or telling the truth. To solve each puzzle you have to construct a question in such a way that you get the information in spite of the difficulty with your informant.

You also have to suspend belief just a little more than before and assume that you are unable to tell whether someone is male or female just by looking at them or talking to them. They all know, but you do not, except by considering the answers to the clever questions you have put to them!

TALS MEN TELL THE TRUTH
TALS FEMALES LIE
FROO MALES LIE
FROO FEMALES TELL THE TRUTH

1   Think of a simple question which you could ask someone so that they only answer "Yes" if they belong to the Froo family.

2   Now think of a question which would only be answered by "Yes" if the person is a member of the Tals family.

44

3   Design a question which would only be answered by "No" if the person is male.

4   Find another question which would only be answered by "No" if the person is female.

5   You are bird watching and come across two men, one Tals and one Froo, but you do know which is which. You know that they are both experts in bird identification and you want to know if the bird that you can all see is a kite or a buzzard. What single question could you ask to establish which it is?

6   Can you think of a question that all four types of person (that is Froo males, Froo females, Tals males and Tals females) will give the same answer to?

7   Think of a question that only a Froo female could answer "No" to.

8   Think of a question that only a Froo male could answer "Yes" to.

9   Can you think of a question that only a Tals male could answer "Yes" to?

10 Can you design a single question to discover both the family and the sex of anyone you ask?

11 Find to questions that you could ask any person to discover both their family and sex. When I say two questions, I mean that one is to be asked after the other and both answers used.

The solutions to the TALKING TO THE TALS AND THE FROOS puzzles are on page 70.

Who is Holding the Card?

This group of puzzles concerns three sisters Annie, Betty and Cassie who can each lie or tell the truth as she pleases. They have invented a logic game which gives rise to some interesting problems.

They have two playing cards, the Ace of Spades and the King of Spades. One of the sisters put their empty hands behind their backs so that no-one else knows who has the card, not which one has been taken.

If the card if the King, then the sister who is holding it must tell the truth. If the card is the Ace, she must lie.

Now for the puzzles!

THE SISTER HOLDING THE ACE LIES
THE SISTER HOLDING THE KING
TELLS THE TRUTH

1 The sisters enter the room with their hands behind their backs.
They make statements as follows:

Annie: I have the card

Betty: I do not have the card.

Cassie: Annie does not have the card.

Given that, at most, one of the three statements is true, who has
the card and what is it?

2   The three walk out of the room and then come back. They may or may not have changed the card but they make the following statements:

   Annie: Betty does not have the card

   Betty: I do not have the card.

   Cassie: I have the card.

Given that, at most, one of the three statements is true and at least one statement is false, who has the card and what is it this time?

3   Again, the sisters walk out of the room and come back. They each make one statement as follows:

   Annie: Betty does not have the card.

   Betty: I do not have the card.

   Cassie: I have the card.

4   The three sisters go out of the room and come back in but this
     time Cassie shows you that she does not have a card behind her
     back. She refuses to make a statement but the other two do so.

     Annie: I do not have the card.

     Betty: Exactly one of these statements is false.

     Does Annie or Betty have the card and which card does it
     have to be?

The solutions to the WHO IS HOLDING THE CARD? puzzles are on page 71.

The Farewell Party

For the final problem we return to the Troo and Fals families who are holding a farewell party. It is for a friend of A's who is about to leave to speak at a Seminar on Logical Thinking.

Eleven people are present and they each make a statement. Four of them, (A, B, J and K) also make a second statement which will help to find out who is telling the truth and who is lying.

TROOS ALWAYS TELL THE TRUTH
FALS ALWAYS LIE

A: J and B are from the same family.

A: My friend is called Alf.

B: A's friend is called Bert.

B: Today is Friday.

C: It is either Saturday or Sunday.

D: H and E are from the same family.

E: A and B are from the same family.

F: Of myself and E, exactly one of us is from the Fals family.

G: Of myself and D, we are either both from the Fals family or both from the Troo family.

H: Either it is Wednesday or A is from the Fals family.

I: At most, 4 people are from the Troo family.

J: It is either Monday or K is from the Fals family.

J: A's friend is called Colin.

K: I and A are from the same family.

K: It is not Tuesday.

You must assume that each person knows which family everyone else comes from. Everyone also knows the name of A's friend and what day of the week it is.

If you are in doubt about "Either-or" statements, see page 61.

The puzzle is to answer these questions:

Which family is each of the guests from?

What day of the week is it?

What is the name of A's friend?

Who should propose the toast wishing the friend a safe journey?

The solution to THE FAREWELL PARTY puzzle is on page 71.

Hints and Solutions

Useful Methods

These logical puzzles can be solved in lots of ways and each person will gradually develop a favourite method. However, here are four different suggestions which may help you to get started.

Method 1: Trying All The Combinations

The first strategy works best in the simpler cases where there are not too many people present. For instance, in the puzzles about the Troo and Fals families, the number of possible combinations to try doubles with each additional person.

If there are two people present, there are four possible combinations.

1. Troo	2. Troo	3. Fals	4. Fals
Troo	Fals	Troo	Fals

What you have to do is to take each combination in turn and examine the statements in the light. For the first combination you must assume that both are telling the truth. Are the statements contradictory or inconsistent? If so, then the assumption must be wrong and you must try the next combination. If both statements are consistent, then you may have found the solution. It is always wise to work through all the combinations to check up on your thinking. It is only too easy to jump to conclusions.

If there are three people present then there are eight possible combinations to examine.

1. TTT	2. TTF	3. TFT	4. FTT
5. TFF	6. FTF	7. FFT	8. FFF

If there are four people present, then there are 16 combinations, and so it continues, doubling with each additional person.

Method 2: Looking For The Special Statement

This strategy can speed up the process by looking to see if one statement really establishes something about a particular speaker. For instance, the statement "I am from the Fals family" can never be said, but "I am from Class 2" immediately establishes beyond doubt that the speaker is from Class 3 and is lying.

This is not, of course, a completely independent strategy from method 1, but is used in conjunction with it. It reduces the number of combinations to try and it is a very satisfying application of logical thinking.

Method 3: The Logical Tree

This strategy takes it name from the fact that the logical possibilities branch out rather like the branches of a tree. What you do is to assume that the first statement is true. Then follow along all the branches leading from it, dealing with each possible combination. You must continue until you reach a contradiction or a solution. If you reach a contradiction, then you know that the first statement is not true and the "true" half of the tree can be eliminated. Then assume that the first statement is false and work along all the branches leading from it until the puzzle is solved.

In very complicated puzzles it may be necessary to make later assumptions and to split the problem into half again.

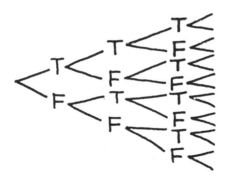

Method 4: The Grid Diagram

This method is not so much a strategy as a convenient way to clarify your ideas. Draw a grid rather like the one below for each puzzle. Devise a system of ticks, crosses or symbols to record the various trials and possibilities. Eliminate those which lead to contradictions and you have the solution to the puzzle.

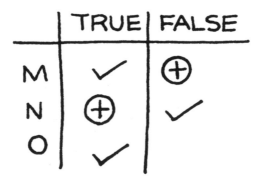

Two Part Statements

Some statements are really two substatements linked by pairs of words such as "Either-or", "Both-and" and "If-then". The truth of such statements depends on the truth or falsehood of the substatements.

1 "Either-or"

Either (PART A) or	(PART B) =	(OVERALL STATEMENT)
True	True	True
True	False	True
False	True	True
False	False	False

This kind of statement is only false if both of the substatements are false. Example:

Either Alf owns the book or he is from the Fals family.

In this example, part A is "Alf owns the book" and part B is " he is from the Fals family". The overall statement is only false if he does not own the book and does not come from the Fals family.

2 "Both-and"

Both	(PART A)	or	(PART B) =	(OVERALL STATEMENT)
	True		True	True
	True		False	False
	False		True	False
	False		False	False

This kind of statement is only true if both of the substatements are true. Example:

Both Olive and Ruth live in the first house.

In this example, part A is "Olive lives in the first house" and part B is "Ruth lives in the first house". The overall statement is only true if they both do in fact live in the same house. Such statements seldom cause difficulty.

3 "If-then"

If	(PART A) or	(PART B)=	(OVERALL STATEMENT)
	True	True	True
	True	False	False
	False	True	Not tested
	False	False	Not tested

None of these puzzles in this book is such that part A of an "if-then" statement is false, so the problem of dealing with a "not-tested" statement is avoided. In more advanced work on logic such statements are regarded as "true", although to people thinking in a simply common sense way this is often hard to accept. Example:

If Fred is from the Troo family, then George is from the Fals family. In this example, part A is "Fred is from the Troo family" and is the condition which must be met if the second part is to be tested. Part B is "George is from the Fals family". The overall statement is true or false according to whether or not George is or is not from the Fals family.

THE SOLUTIONS

The Two Families

1 Alan is from the Fals family and Bert is from the Troo family.
2 Christine's family cannot be worked out, but Daphne comes from the Fals family.
3 Ernie's family cannot be worked out but Fred belongs to the Troo family.
4 Hilda is from the Fals family. It is not possible to work out which family Gertrude comes from.
5 Neither's family can be determined.
6 Karen and Laura are both from the Fals family.
7 Mark is from the Troo family and Neil is from the Fals family.

More About The Families

1 A is from the Troo family. B's family cannot be determined.
2 C is from the Troo family, D is from the Fals family.
3 The only think you can say about E and F is that they are both from the same family.
4 This time, the only thing that can be said is that they are both from the same family.

5   I is from the Troo family, J is from the Fals family.
6   The answers are in fact the same as question 5.
7   K is from the Troo family, L is from the Fals family.
8   M belongs to the Troo family, so does N. N's statement is necessary. If M is not from the Troo family, then the condition is not met. See page 63.
9   Yes, O and P are both from the Fals family.
10 Q is from the Fals family. R and S are from the Troo family.
11 T is from the Troo family, U is from the Fals family and V is from the Troo family.
12 W is from the Troo family, X is from the Fals family and Y is from the Troo family.
13 Z is from the Troo family, ZA is from the Fals family and ZB is from the Troo family.
14 The only thing that is certain is that ZD is from the Fals family. ZC and ZE could be from either family.
15 ZH is from the Troo family.
16 ZK is from the Fals family.
17 ZN is from the Fals family.
18 ZQ is from the Troo family. Yes, both are from the Fals family.

Classes 1, 2 and 3

A good way to tackle these problems is start by making a table of what someone can say about himself or herself. For instance, a member of Class 1 can say "I am from Class 1" or "I am not from Class 2" or "I am not from Class 3", but cannot say anything else beginning with "I am". Likewise a member of Class 2 can make three statements, but a member of Class 3 can make six. Then start each puzzle by looking first at those statements which use the words "I" or "me".

1　A is from class 1, B is from class 2 and C is from class 3.
2　D is from class 1, E is from class 3, and F is from class 2.
3　G is from class 3, H is from class and I is a member of class 1.
4　J is from class 3, K is a member of class 2 and L is from class 1.
5　M is from class 1, N is from class 2 and O is from class 3.
6　M is from class 1, N is from class 2 and O is from class 3.
7　S is from class 1, T is a member of class 3 and U is from class 2.
8　This time S is from class 3, T is a member of class 2 and U is a member of class 1.
9　V is from class 2, W is from class 3 and X is from class 1.

Whose Room is it?

1   It is B's room and he is from the Troo family.
2   It is D's room and she does not tell the truth.
3   It is E's room. He is from the Troo family.
4   It is G's room and she is from the Fals family.
5   Yes and he is from the Troo family, so he always tells the truth.
6   The room belongs to L and he is from the Troo family.
7   It is N's room and he or she is from the Fals family. Yes, it is possible
         because they are both Troos.
8   The rule I worked out was that everyone from the Troo family lives in a
         room with a prime number and veryone from the Fals family lives in
         the other rooms. You may have found a better rule. The answers are
         as follows:

a.   The occupant of room 11 is from the Troo family (because 11 is a
         prime number).
b.   The prime numbers up to 30 are , 3, 5, 7, 11, 13, 17, 19, 23 and
         29. There are 10 of them so the answer is that there are 10 people
         from the Troo family on the island.

I have excluded room 1 because some people call it prime (I do not) and
may have a different answer.

Who does it Belong to?

1. The ruler belongs to C.
2. E owns the football.
3. H owns the pencil.
4. This puzzle cannot be solved. Notice that I did ask if you could solve it, not what the answer was.
5. O owns the book.
6. Q owns the lunch box.

The Tals and The Froos

1. A is a Tals female.
2. B is a Froo male.
3. C is a Froo female.
4. All you can say about D is that he is male.
5. All you can say here is that E is from the Froo family.
6. F is female.
7. G is from the Tals family.
8. H is male and I is female and they both come from the same family. It is not possible to say which.
9. J & K are both Froo males.
10. L is a Tals female and M is a Froo male.

John and his Twin

1   Ask either of them, "Is John truthful today?" If the answer that you get is "Yes" then you are speaking to John. An answer of "No" means you are speaking to John's brother.

2   Ask either of them, "Are you John?" A "Yes" that John is truthful on the day the question is asked. A "No" answer means that John's brother is truthful that day.

3   There are several questions that you could ask. One example is, "If I asked your brother today if his name was Mark, would he say yes?" Another good question is, "Of the two statements, 'You are lying today' and 'Your brother's name is Marcus', is one and only one of them true?"

4   Ask her, "Are you an elephant?" twice. Is the answers are "Yes, yes" she always lies. If they are "No, no" then she tells the truth all the time. If the answers are "Yes, no" or "No, yes" then she alternates with her statements. You could also ask a question to which the answer is obvious twice, for example, "Am I asking you a question?" or "Does 2 plus 2 equal 4?"

Yes, you can always find out which is John.

Talking to the Tals and the Froos

1 Simply ask "Are you female?"

2 Ask "Are you male?"

3 Ask "are you from the Froo family?"

4 "Are you from the Tals family?" would work.

5 Would you friend say that the bird we can see is a kite? If the answer is
      "yes", then the bird is a buzzard. If "no" then it is a kite.

6 "Do you always tell the truth?" would always be answered with "Yes" and
      "Do you always lie?" would get a "No" answer from all of the four
      types.

7 Ask "Are you a Tals male?"

8 "Are you a Tals female?" is a question that only a Froo male could answer
      "Yes" to.

9 Say "Are you not a Froo female? Or " You are not a Froo female,
      Do you agree?"

10 It is not possible to ask a single question to determine full information
       about any of the four types. There are four types and only two
       possible answers.

11 "Are you male?" and "Are you from the Tals family?" are two questions
       that will work. There are many variations on this. The general solution

is that one question is "Are you X?" where X is male or female and the other question is "Are you from the Y family?" where Y is Tals or Froo.

Who is Holding the Card?

1   Betty has the card. It is the Ace.
2   Annie has the card. It is the King.
3   Cassie has the card. It is the King.
4   Annie has the card. It is the Ace.

The Farewell Party

This puzzle is not as hard as it looks if you solve it the right way. Let us first look at F's statement. If it is true then E must be from the Fals family (because it is the case that exactly one of the two is from the Fals family and we know that F is not). If it is false then E is still from the Fals family (because as it is not the case that exactly one is from the Fals family, the two must be either both from the Fals family or both from the Troo family and, since F is already from the Fals family, E must also be from the Fals family). In both cases E is from the Fals family. Next, look at G's statement. In both cases this time, D is from the Troo family (I leave the proof to you).

D's statement is therefore true and it is the case that H and E are from the same family. As E is from the Fals family, H must also be from the Fals family. To make this statement false, both parts of it have to be false. So it is not Wednesday and A is from the Troo family. We now know the following:

A – Troo family   E – Fals family
D – Troo family   H – Fals family

Today is not Wednesday.

As A is from the Troo family, both his statements are true so we can now say that A's friend is called Alf. This means that B and J are both from the Fals family because they both imply that A's friend is not called Alf. B's second statement is also false so it is not Friday. J's first statement is false so it is not Monday and K is from the Troo family. It is not Tuesday and I and A are therefore from the same family and I must be from the Troo family because we know A is. We now know the following:

A – Troo family   E – Fals family   J – Fals family
B – Fals family   H – Fals family   K – Troo family
D – Troo family   I – Troo family
A's friend is called Alf.
Today is not Wednesday, Friday, Monday or Tuesday.

I's statement is true, so, at most four people are from the Troo family. We already have four people from the Troo family (A, D, I and K), so everyone else must be from the Tals family. C's statement is false so today is not Saturday or Sunday and the only remaining day is Thursday. We now solved the puzzle! The solution is:

A – Troo family
B – Fals family
C – Fals family
D – Troo family

E – Fals family
F – Fals family
H – Fals family
I – Troo family

J – Fals family
K – Troo family

Today is Thursday
A's friend is called Alf.
Wishes for a safe journey are best made by someone who tells the truth. It could be A, D, I or K.

Paradoxical Pictures

Throughout this book there are some puzzle-like pictures which are rather confusing. They pose questions which have an element of absurdity about them. Some may seem impossible to answer at all. For instance, one might reasonably ask if it possible not to read a notice asking you not to read it! By the time you have read it, it is already too late.

Some of the pictures are illustrations of paradoxes. The definition of a paradox is that it is a self-contradictory statement which seems essentially absurd and which conflicts with the notion of what is reasonable or possible.

A well-known paradox takes the form of a question.

What happens when an irresistible force meets and immovable object?

If a force is irresistible, then nothing can resist it. If an object is immovable then nothing can move it. Both entities cannot exist in the same Universe and so the question cannot ever be answered.

A puzzling logical paradox is as follows:

Is "No" the answer to this question?

If you say "Yes" that "No" is the correct answer then "No" really should be the correct answer. If you answer "No", then you imply that "No" is not the correct answer and that it should be "Yes". This is impossible and therefore the question is a paradox.

Some statements sound like paradoxes, but really are just rather confusing statements. Consider this one.

I always lie.

If this statement is true, then this statement is also a lie and it means that on at least one occasion he has told the truth. If he is not telling the truth now, this means that he has told the truth on at least one occasion. Hence this is a simply a statement which is untrue, and not a paradox.

Each of the pictures poses a question or makes a statement which demands clear thinking. Is it a true paradox or not? If not, is the statement true or untrue? Who is telling the truth?

See what else is on offer at www.tarquinbooks.com